Stage 1

Kipper Stories

Maoliosa Kelly

Teaching

Contents

At School

Getting Up

Look Out!

The Haircut

The Lost Teddy

The Library

Introduction

Stage 1 of Oxford Reading Tree is the first stage in the reading programme. It concentrates on developing the early reading skills that children need to become competent readers. Stage 1 includes twelve wordless books and six caption books.

Six of the Stage 1 wordless stories feature the character of Kipper. A further six feature Biff and Chip. The stories reflect children's own experiences: the first day at nursery school, losing a favourite toy, getting a haircut. The children quickly identify with the characters and their experiences and this motivates them to find out more about the family and their friends by reading the other stories in the series.

The wordless books at Stage 1 allow children to learn how stories work, including the order and direction in which they are read. Children are encouraged to look at the illustrations to find out what is happening in the story. By telling the story in their own words they learn to use all the information they derive from the illustrations, and develop their oral skills.

How to introduce the books

Before reading the story for guided and independent reading, always read the title and talk about the picture on the front cover. Go through the book with the children, looking at the pictures and talking about them. Prompts and ideas are provided for introducing each story to the child or with a group of children.

The booklet provides you with suggestions for using the books in groups for guided, group and independent activities, matched to text, sentence and word level objectives. There are also separate guided reading cards available for six titles at each stage. If there are context words (listed in the chart on page 4) that are new or unfamiliar, point them out and read them with the children. Suggestions are also provided for speaking and listening activities, writing activities, and cross-curricular links.

Take-Home Cards are also available for each book. These provide friendly prompts and suggestions for parents reading with their children at home. You can store the relevant card with each book in your "Take-Home" selection of titles.

Reading skills

Stage 1 is essential for:
- introducing the main characters
- encouraging children to talk about themselves and their experiences in relation to the stories
- developing a positive attitude towards reading
- teaching initial book handling skills
- developing listening skills
- introducing the first key words
- developing an understanding of the story.

Vocabulary chart

At School	Year R High frequency words	at
	Context words	school
Getting Up	Year R High frequency words	up
	Context words	getting
Look Out!	Year R High frequency words	look
	Context words	out
The Haircut	Year R High frequency words	the
	Context words	haircut
The Lost Teddy	Year R High frequency words	the
	Context words	lost teddy
The Library	Year R High frequency words	the
	Context words	library

Curriculum coverage chart

	Speaking and listening	Reading	Writing
At School			
NLS/NC	1e, 2e, 3e, 4a	W2, S3, S4, T1	T12
Scotland	Level A	Level A	Level A
N.Ireland	Activities: b, e, h Outcomes: a, e	Activities: c, f Outcomes: b, c, e	Outcomes: a, f, g
Wales	Range: 1, 3, 5 Skills: 3, 4, 5	Range: 1, 4, 5, 6 Skills: 1, 2	Range: 2, 4 Skills: 2, 3
Getting Up			
NLS/NC	11a	W11, S4, T1, T9	T15
Scotland	Level A	Level A	Level A
N.Ireland	Activities: b, e, g, h Outcomes: a, e	Activities: c, f Outcomes: b, c, e	Outcomes: a, f, g
Wales	Range: 1, 3, 5 Skills: 3, 4, 5	Range: 1, 4, 5, 6 Skills: 1, 2	Range: 2, 3, 4 Skills: 2, 3, 5
Look Out!			
NLS/NC	8c	W2, W6, S3, T1, T7, T9	T11
Scotland	Level A	Level A	Level A
N.Ireland	Activities: b, e, f, h Outcomes: a, e	Activities: c, f Outcomes: b, c, e	Outcomes: a, f, g
Wales	Range: 1, 3, 5 Skills: 3, 4, 5	Range: 1, 4, 5, 6 Skills: 1, 2	Range: 2, 3 Skills: 2, 3, 6
The Haircut			
NLS/NC	11a	W11, S3, T1	T11
Scotland	Level A	Level A	Level A
N.Ireland	Activities: b, e, f, g, h Outcomes: a, h	Activities: a, c, f, g Outcomes: b, c, e	Outcomes: a, f, g
Wales	Range: 1, 3, 5 Skills: 3, 4, 5	Range: 1, 4, 5, 6 Skills: 1, 2	Range: 2, 3, 4 Skills: 2, 3
The Lost Teddy			
NLS/NC	8c	W6, S3, T1, T7	T12
Scotland	Level A	Level A	Level A
N.Ireland	Activities: b, e, g, h Outcomes: a, h	Activities: a, c, f Outcomes: b, c, e	Outcomes: a, f, g
Wales	Range: 1, 2, 3 Skills: 3, 4, 5	Range: 1, 4, 5, 6 Skills: 1, 2	Range: 2, 3 Skills: 2, 3
The Library			
NLS/NC	1d, 1e, 1f, 3a, 3e, 4a	W3, S3, S4, T1	T12
Scotland	Level A	Level A	Level A
N.Ireland	Activities: b, e, g Outcomes: a, h	Activities: c, e, f Outcomes: a, b, c, e	Outcomes: a, f, g
Wales	Range: 1, 2, 3 Skills: 3, 4, 5	Range: 1, 4, 5, 6 Skills: 1, 2	Range: 2, 3 Skills: 2, 3

At School

Before reading

- Read the title and show the picture on the cover. Ask the children: *Where is Kipper? What is he doing?*
- Look at page 1. Ask: *Does Kipper want to go to school?*
- Look through the rest of the book and ask for each page: *What is happening here?*
  How do you think Kipper feels?
- Look at page 8. Ask: *Does Kipper want to go home now?*
- Ask the children to talk about their own experiences.

During reading

- Ask the children to look through the book and tell the story in their own words. Prompt them to talk about how Kipper's feelings change.

Observing Check that the children:
- use the terms about books correctly (T1)
- hold the book the right way up
- open the book and "read" it from left to right.

Group and independent reading activities

Text level work

Objective To understand and use correctly terms about books: book, cover, beginning, end, page, title (T1).

- Ask: *Can you show me the cover of the book? What is the title? What happened at the beginning of the story? What happened at the end of the story? Show me the page where Kipper plays with the cooker.*

Are the children able to refer to the right part of the book, e.g. the beginning and the end, automatically?

Sentence level work

Objectives That words are ordered left to right and need to be read that way to make sense (S3); to use capital letter for the start of own name (S4).

You will need the sentence below written on the board:
Kipper is at school.

● Ask the children to read the sentence aloud as you point to each word from left to right. Then ask the children to substitute Kipper's name for the name of some of the children in the class.

Observing Do the children read the correct word as you point to it?

Word level work

Objective To hear and identify initial sounds in words (W2).

● Ask the children to look at pages 2 and 3 of the storybook and find three things that begin with the sound "k" (Kipper, car, coat).

Observing Do the children correctly identify objects that begin with "k"?

Speaking and listening activities

Objectives Include relevant detail (1e); ask questions to clarify their understanding (2e); give reasons for their opinion (3e); through drama, explore characters and emotions (4a).

You will need a teddy.

● Ask one child to pretend to be Kipper in the story. The child playing the part of Kipper should hold Kipper's teddy. The other children in the class have to think up questions to ask Kipper about how he felt on his first day at nursery school.

Writing

Objective To experiment with writing in a variety of play situations (T12).

You will need a variety of drawing materials: paper, crayons or coloured pencils.

- Talk to the children about their experiences of their first day at nursery school, what they did and what they played at.
- Ask the children to draw a picture of themselves on their first day at nursery school.
- Ask the children to write a caption under their picture using their own name. The caption should read "X at school".
- Ask the child to show you which is the picture and which is the writing.

Getting Up

Getting Up

Before reading

- Read the title and show the cover picture. Ask the children: *Who is getting up?*
  Have you ever got up early on special days?
- Look through the book and ask what each character is doing.
- Ask: *What time is it on the clock?*
  What is Biff carrying?
  Who is coming to the house?
  Why did the children get up so early?
- Ask the children to describe how Dad feels.

During reading

- Ask the children to look through the book and tell the story in their own words. Prompt them to talk about how Kipper felt in the story.

Observing Check that the children:
- use the terms about books correctly: book, cover (T1)
- hold the book the right way up
- open the book and "read" it from left to right.

Group and independent reading activities

Text level work

Objective To be aware of story structures, e.g. actions/reactions, consequences, and the ways that stories are built up and concluded (T9).

- Ask the children: *At the beginning of the story did you think that the story was going to be about a normal morning when Kipper got up?*
  What clues were there in the story that this was not a normal morning?
  Do you think that the children planned this in advance? How do you know?

Do you think that Dad knew or do you think it was a surprise for him?
Do you think Mum knew about the plan?

Observing Are the children able to identify what is different from a normal morning in the story?

Sentence level work

Objective To use a capital letter for start of own name (S4).

You will need paper and pencils.

- Ask the children to draw a picture of themselves on their birthday and write their name underneath.

Observing Do the children use a capital letter for the start of their name?

Word level work

Objective To make collections of significant words and words linked to particular topics (birthdays) (W11).

You will need the following word cards: Kipper, Happy, Birthday; cards of each month of the year.

- Ask the children to put the word cards in the correct order, i.e. Happy Birthday Kipper.
- Arrange the month cards in a sequence across the room.
- Ask the children to stand in front of the month of their birthday.
- Count how many children have birthdays in each month.
- Make a chart of the months and write the total number of birthdays in each month.
- Ask the children which month has the most birthdays and which month has the least birthdays.

Observing Can the children read the character's name with confidence? Do they correctly sequence "Happy" and "Birthday"?

Cross-curricular links

◄► Maths: solve a relevant problem by using simple lists, tables and charts to sort, classify and organise information.

Speaking and listening activities

Objective Working in role (11a).

- Ask one child to play the part of Dad. The other children have to sing "Happy Birthday" to Dad and Dad has to blow out the candles on his cake.
- Ask another child to pretend to be Kipper and repeat the exercise, asking the children to sing "Happy Birthday" to Kipper.

Writing

Objective To use writing to communicate in a variety of ways, incorporating it into play and everyday classroom life, e.g. greetings cards (T15).

You will need a selection of paper, coloured pencils, crayons and a birthday card.

- Show the children a birthday card and talk about the cover with the salutation and the picture. Look inside the card and show the children where it says "To" and "From".
- Put the children into pairs and ask them to write and draw a birthday card for the other child in their pair.

Look Out!

Before reading

- Read the title and ask the children: *When would you say this?* Explain the exclamation mark and ask the children to read the title dramatically.
- Show the cover picture and ask: *What is Kipper going to do?*
- Look through the story. Ask: *Do you think Kipper is being naughty? What does he not do well on his bike? How do Biff and Chip help?*
- Talk about road safety and the things you need to do to ride a bike safely.

During reading

- Ask the children to look through the book and tell the story in their own words.

Observing Check that the children:
- use the terms about books correctly (T1)
- hold the book the right way up
- open the book and "read" it from left to right
- anticipate consequences of actions (T9).

Group and independent reading activities

Text level work

Objective To use knowledge of familiar texts to re-tell to others, recounting the main points in correct sequence (T7).

- Ask: *What did Kipper do at the beginning of the story? What was the first naughty thing Kipper did? What was the second naughty thing Kipper did? What was the third naughty thing Kipper did? What did the family do at the end?*

Sentence level work

Objective   That words are ordered left to right and need to be read that way to make sense (S3).

You will need the sentence below written on the board:
Look out!

●   Ask the children to read the sentence aloud as you point to each word from left to right. Encourage them to read with expression, as if they were shouting a warning to Kipper.

Observing   Do the children read the correct word as you point to it?

Word level work

Objectives   To read on sight the high frequency word "look" (W6); to hear and identify initial sounds in words (W2).

●   Write the words "Look out!" on the board and ask the children to tell you which word says "look". Ask the children what sound begins with "l" and what sound ends with "k". Can they think of some other words that start with "l"? Can they think of words that rhyme with "look"? (book, cook, rook, took)

Observing   Do the children correctly identify the word "look"?

Speaking and listening activities

Objective   Describe events and experiences (8c).

You will need a bicycle helmet.

●   Ask one child to pretend to be Kipper and wear the bicycle helmet.
●   Ask the child to describe what happened to Kipper in the story and how he felt as he crashed into things.
●   Ask the children to make suggestions for a list of rules for riding a bike safely.

Cross-curricular link

◄► PSHE: rules for, and ways of, keeping safe, including basic road safety.

Writing

Objective To understand that writing remains constant, i.e. will always "say" the same thing (T11).

You will need photocopies of pages with blank speech bubbles, pencils, scissors

● Ask the children to write in the speech bubbles the words "Look out!"
● Then ask them to cut out the speech bubbles.
● Ask them to turn to pages 2 and 3, decide which character is saying "Look out!" and position the speech bubble above the character's head. The children could do the same thing for pages 4 and 5, and 6 and 7.

The Haircut

Before reading

- Read the title and show the picture on the cover. Ask the children: *Who do you think needs a haircut?*
- Ask: *Who cuts your hair? Do you like getting your hair cut?*
- Look through the story and talk about why Kipper needs a haircut. Ask: *Where does he go to get his hair cut? Who else gets his hair cut?*
- Turn to page 8. *What do Kipper and Dad think of their haircuts? What does Mum think of them?*

During reading

- Ask the children to look through the book and tell the story in their own words.

Observing Check that the children:

- use the terms about books correctly: book, cover, beginning, end, page, title (T1)
- hold the book the right way up
- open the book and "read it" from left to right.

Group and independent reading activities

Text level work

Objective To recognise printed and handwritten words in a variety of settings (T1).

- Turn to pages 2 and 3. Ask: *Can you tell me the name of the hairdresser's where Kipper goes?*
  Can you point to the word "shampoo" on a bottle in the window?
  What do you think the other bottles say?
  What time is the hairdresser's open on Saturday?

Do the children go to the correct part of the picture to locate the relevant information?

Do they use the information in the picture or their knowledge of the context to guess the answers?

Sentence level work

Objective That words are ordered left to right and need to be read that way to make sense (S3).

You will need the sentence below written on the board:

Kipper got a haircut.

● Ask the children to read the sentence aloud as you point to each word from left to right. Then ask the children to substitute Kipper's name for the name of some of the children in the class.

Observing Do the children read the correct word as you point to it?

Word level work

Objective To make collections of words linked to particular topics (W11).

● Ask the children to look at pages 6 and 7 of the storybook and find any words which begin with the sound "h" (hairdresser, hair, hairbrush, hairspray). Ask them to draw pictures of all the things that begin with the sound "h". What else do they notice about this collection of words? (They all begin with the word "hair".)

Observing Do the children correctly identify objects that begin with the sound "h"?

Speaking and listening activities

Objective Working in role (11a).

● Ask the children to work in pairs. Ask one child to be the hairdresser and the other to be the customer. The child playing the customer describes how he/she wants his/her hair cut. The child playing the hairdresser has to ask questions to find out how the customer wants his or her hair cut.

- Discuss how hair grows and needs to be cut. Talk about other parts of the body that grow and need to be cut, e.g. nails.
- Discuss the different hair colours of the children in the class and how many variations there are (dark, fair, or red).
- Carry out a survey of different hair colours in the class. Ask the children to form into lines according to the colour of their hair.
- Count the number of children in each line and together make a chart on the board.

Cross-curricular link

◀▶ Maths: use a chart to classify and organise information

Writing

Objective To distinguish between writing and drawing (T11).

You will need paper, pencils, crayons and coloured pencils. Write the words, "The Haircut" on the board for the children to copy.

- Ask the children to draw a picture of themselves with a haircut they would like to have.
- Ask them to write their name at the top of the picture.
- Ask them to write the words "The Haircut" at the bottom of the page.

The Lost Teddy

Before reading

● Read the title and show the cover picture. Ask the children: *What is Kipper carrying?*
● Ask if they have ever lost a toy. How did they feel?
● Look through the book and ask: *What is Kipper thinking?*
 What has happened to Teddy?
 How does Kipper feel?
 How do Biff and Chip try to help?
 Where do Mum and Kipper go?
● Look at page 8. Ask: *How does Kipper feel now?*

During reading

● Ask the children to look through the book and tell the story in their own words. Encourage them to use story language. Prompt them to talk about how Kipper felt.

Observing Check that the children:
 ■ use the terms about books correctly (T1)
 ■ hold the book the right way up
 ■ open the book and "read" it from left to right.

Group and independent reading activities

Text level work

Objective To use knowledge of familiar texts to re-tell to others, recounting the main points in correct sequence (T7).

● Ask: *What happened on the first day of the story?*
 How did Kipper lose his teddy?
 What happened that night? How did Kipper feel?
 What happened the next day?
 What happened at the end of the story?

Are the children able to retell the story in the correct sequence? Can they identify which events happened on which day?

Sentence level work

Objective That words are ordered left to right and need to be read that way to make sense (S3).

You will need the sentence below written on the board:

Kipper lost his teddy.

● Ask the children to read the sentence aloud as you point to each word from left to right. Then ask the children to substitute Kipper's name for the name of some of the children in the class.

Observing Do the children read the correct word as you point to it?

Word level work

Objective To read on sight the high frequency word "the" (W6).

You will need six cards with the word "the" written on them.

● Hide the word cards around the classroom. Ask the children to find them. When somebody finds a card ask him/her what is written on it.

Observing Do the children read the word "the" on the card when they find it?

Speaking and listening activities

Objective Describe events and experiences (8c).

● Ask the children to work in groups of three. Turn to pages 4 and 5 of the storybook and ask the children to act out this scene. One child pretends to be Kipper and the other two pretend to be Biff and Chip. "Kipper" describes to "Biff " and "Chip" what happened to Teddy and how he feels. "Biff" and "Chip" try to comfort "Kipper".

- Ask the children how they think Teddy feels when he gets left on the bus. Then ask: *How do you think Teddy felt when Kipper found him again?*

Cross-curricular links

◀▶ PSHE: developing good relationships and respecting the differences between people

Writing

Objective To write captions for pictures and drawings (T12).

You will need paper, pencils, crayons, and coloured pencils.

- Ask the children to draw a picture of Teddy when he was lost. Ask them to write the words "The Lost Teddy" at the bottom of the picture. Tell the children that they can copy the words from the front cover of the storybook.

The Library

Before reading

- Read the title and show the cover picture. Ask the children: *Have you ever been to a library?*
  How many books could you take out?
  What happens if you take the books back late?
- Look through the book together asking: *Why is Dad giving the librarian some money?*
  Where does Kipper go?
  How many books does he want to take out?
- Look at page 8. Ask: *How many books do Dad and Kipper take out?*
  Why does the librarian look unhappy?

During reading

- Ask the children to look through the book and tell the story in their own words.

Observing Check that the children:
- use the terms about books correctly (T1)
- hold the book the right way up
- open the book and "read" it from left to right.

Group and independent reading activities

Text level work

Objective To understand and use correctly terms about books and print: book, cover, beginning, end, page, word, letter, title (T1).

- Ask: *Can you show me the cover of the book? What is the title?*
  Can you show me the author's name?
  Can you show me the illustrator's name?
  What happened at the beginning of the story?
  What did Kipper do in the library?
  What happened at the end of the story?

Are the children able to refer to the right part of the book, e.g. the beginning and the end, automatically?

Sentence level work

Objectives That words are ordered left to right and need to be read that way to make sense (S3); to use a capital letter at the start of own name (S4).

You will need the sentence below written on the board:

Kipper went to the library.

- Ask the children to read the sentence aloud as you point to each word from left to right.
- Ask: *Does the "K" always look like that?* Explain that it is a capital letter because it is the beginning of a name. Show the children what a lower case letter "k" looks like by writing it on the board.
- Ask the children to re-read the sentence substituting Kipper's name for the names of children in the class.

Observing Do the children read the correct word as you point to it?

Word level work

Objective Understanding alphabetical order through alphabet books, rhymes and songs (W3).

You will need an alphabet frieze; tabletop alphabets.

- Sing the alphabet song to the tune of Auld Lang Syne. As the children sing the song, point to each letter of the alphabet along the frieze.
- Put the children into groups and ask them to put their surnames into alphabetical order. They can refer to table top alphabets to help them.

Speaking and listening activities

Objectives Focus on the main point (1d); include relevant detail (1e); take into account the needs of their listeners (1f); take turns in speaking (3a); give reasons for their opinions (3e); use language and actions to convey situations and characters (4a).

- Ask each child in a group to recommend a story they have read giving one good reason why the other children should read the book.
- Ask the group to play "libraries". One child in each group should be the librarian. Others "borrow" a book each from the class library which they take to the librarian who will "stamp" it and allow them to take it home.

Writing

Objective To experiment with writing in a variety of play situations (T12).

You will need one A4 sheet of paper per child, folded into four to make a booklet; coloured pencils and crayons.

- Give each child a booklet and ask them to design their own book cover. Each child should draw a picture on the cover, write in the title and their own name as the author. If they have time, they could also design the back cover. The children can look at some real book covers for ideas. These booklets can be used in the librarian role play activity in the Speaking and Listening section above.

Oxford Reading Tree resources at this level

There is a range of material available at a similar level to these stories which can be used for consolidation or extension.

Stage 1

Teacher support
- Teacher's Handbook
- Big Talkabout Cards
- Big Book for each story
- Guided Reading Cards for three Kipper and Biff and Chip Stories and three First Words Stories
- Take-Home Card for each story
- Extended Stories
- First Storytapes
- Sequencing Cards Photocopy Masters
- ORT Games Stages 1–3
- Group Activity Sheets Book 1 Stages 1–3
- Fact Finder Topic Starters
- My Word Book
- Workbook 1
- Rubber Stamps

Further reading
- Branch Library – Wildsmith Books Stage 1 Pack A

Electronic
- First Story Rhymes
- Clip Art
- Clip and Explore and First Talking Stories
- ORT Online www.OxfordReadingTree.com

For developing phonological awareness
- Alphabet frieze, Tabletop Alphabet Mats, Alphabet Photocopy Masters
- Card Games

OXFORD
UNIVERSITY PRESS

Great Clarendon Street, Oxford OX2 6DP

Oxford University Press is a department of the University of Oxford. It furthers the University's objective of excellence in research, scholarship, and education by publishing worldwide in

Oxford New York

Auckland Cape Town Dar es Salaam Hong Kong Karachi Kuala Lumpur Madrid Melbourne Mexico City Nairobi New Delhi Shanghai Taipei Toronto

With offices in

Argentina Austria Brazil Chile Czech Republic France Greece Guatemala Hungary Italy Japan Poland Portugal Singapore South Korea Switzerland Thailand Turkey Ukraine Vietnam

Oxford is a registered trade mark of Oxford University Press in the UK and in certain other countries

© Oxford University Press 2003

The moral rights of the author have been asserted

Database right Oxford University Press (maker)

First published 2003

British Library Cataloguing in Publication Data

Data available

Cover illustrations Alex Brychta

Teacher's Notes: ISBN-13: 978-0-19-845009-2
ISBN-10: 0-19-845009-5

10 9 8 7

Page make-up by IFA Design Ltd, Plymouth Devon

Printed in China by Imago